Skateboarding

Published by Creative Education

P.O. Box 227, Mankato, Minnesota 56002

Creative Education is an imprint of The Creative Company

Design and production by Blue Design, Portland, Maine

Printed in the United States of America

Photographs by Getty Images (National Geographic, Photonica, Reportage, Stone, Taxi, Taxi Japan)

Library of Congress Cataloging-in-Publication Data

Fandel, Jennifer.

Skateboarding / by Jennifer Fandel.

p. cm. — (Active sports)

Includes index.

ISBN-13: 978-1-58341-469-9

1. Skateboarding—Juvenile literature. I. Title.

GV859.8.F36 2007

796.22—dc22   2006018704

First Edition

9 8 7 6 5 4 3 2 1

Skateboarding

Jennifer Fandel

People started skateboarding about 50 years ago.

You roll down the sidewalk. The wheels under your feet click. Then they clack. You push your foot against the ground. Riding a skateboard is fun!

Skateboards are boards with four wheels. They are made of wood and plastic. Skateboards come in all sorts of colors. Some are red. Others are blue. Some are green.

Skateboard wheels are made of hard plastic.

Lots of people ride skateboards. They are called skaters. Most skaters are kids and teenagers. Some skaters ride alone. Others meet friends. They take turns showing what they can do.

It can be fun to skateboard with friends.

Shoes "grip" a skateboard's rough top.

Skaters stand on their skateboards. The top of a skateboard is rough. It feels like sandpaper. This makes it easy to stand on.

A person needs good balance to skateboard.

Skaters push one foot against the ground. This makes the skateboard's wheels move. Some skaters skate slowly. Others skate very fast!

Some skaters ride their skate-boards to get places. Lots of skaters ride for fun. A few skaters ride in **competitions** (*kom-puh-TISH-uhns*). Tony Hawk was a good skater. He won a lot of competitions.

Some people travel around using skateboards.

Many good skateboarders like to do jumps.

Some people ride skateboards in towns. They ride on the sidewalk. Some skaters do **tricks**. They jump over **curbs**. They slide down railings. They even jump down stairs!

Skateparks are playgrounds for skateboarders.

Some skaters ride their skateboards at skateparks. Skateparks are parks just for skaters. There are ramps to skate on at skateparks. There are curved walls, too. Kids can take skateboarding lessons at skateparks.

Skateboarding can be **dangerous**. New skaters fall down a lot. Skaters trying new tricks fall a lot, too. Most skaters wear a helmet. Lots of skaters wear kneepads. Some wear elbow pads.

Skateboarders should wear a helmet to stay safe.

Skaters practice a lot. Some skaters practice on grass. Others practice on carpet. It does not hurt as much to fall on grass or carpet. And if skaters fall, they get up and try again!

Good skateboarding takes lot of practice!

GLOSSARY

competitions—contests to see who can skate the best

curbs—the edges of sidewalks

dangerous—not safe

tricks—special moves, such as jumps and turns

INDEX